Beyond "The Secret Hand"
(Despues de "La Mano Secreta")

A Comprehensive Guide for Hand Drummers
(Una guía comprehensiva para el percusionista)

By:
Héctor "Pocho" Neciosup
&
José Rosa

Foreword by Glen Caruba

Front and back cover photos © 2007 Contemporary Latin Music Educators, LLC.
Drum photos courtesy of the Pearl Drum Corporation
Book cover and layout by Design Associates

All sound recordings are trademarked and/or copyrighted by
Contemporary Latin Music Educators, LLC.

ISBN 13: 978-1-57424-226-3
ISBN 10: 1-57424-226-1

CENTERSTREAM

THIS BOOK IS DEDICATED TO:

Giovanni Hidalgo
David "La Mole" Ortiz
Miguel Anga Diaz (R.I.P.)
Paoli Mejias

Index/ Índice
PLUS CD TRACK LIST

Foreword / Prólogo...Pg. 6

Preface / Prólogo...Pg. 7

About Authors / Sobre los Autores...Pg. 8

Introduction/ Introducción...Pg. 12
    CD TRACK 1

Chapter 1/ Capitulo 1...Pg. 13
    Beyond "La Mano Secreta"
    Después de "La Mano Secreta"

Chapter 2/ Capitulo 2...Pg. 23
    Rudiments: Exercise to develop independence
    Rudimentos: Ejercicios para desarrollar independencia

Chapter 3/ Capitulo 3...Pg. 27
    Hand Drum Etudes with Clave
    Estudios para "Hand Drum" con la clave

Chapter 4/ Capitulo 4...Pg. 31
    Afro-Caribbean Rhythms
    Ritmos Afro-Caribeños

    CD TRACKS:
    2. Guaguano (Pg, 32)
    3. Guaguano fast (Pg. 32)
    4. Pilon (Pg. 35)
    5. Mozambique (Pg. 35)
    6. Rumba Columbia (Pg. 35)
    7. Afro-Rican 6/8 (Pg. 38)
    8. Merenque (Pg. 37)
    9. Bomba (Pg. 33)
    10. Plena (Pg. 34)
    11. Orisa (Pg. 34)
    12. Songo, slow tempo (Pg. 33)
    13. Songo, fast tempo (Pg. 33)
    14. Performance, Vamos a Gozar

Conclusion & Credits...Pg. 38

Foreword

I first met Hector "Pocho" Neciosup in 1988 when I was a senior in high school. This was eight years into the Cuban immigration and the music, now ingrained into the Miami culture, was steering me into a direction like a soulful magnet and "Pocho" was divinely the engineer to my future. The scene was a small drum shop in Miami, called Resurrection Drums which was a chaotic marketplace of Latin and Drum instruments with no rhyme or reason to organization yet it all seemed to flow quite organically. The success as a business was not that the prices were competitive or everything was in stock, but it was the hang! The store closed at 6:00 but each afternoon as the drummers with "day jobs" got off work and musicians were gearing up for their evening gigs, Resurrection Drums became the scene to jam, socialize, drink Cuban Coffee (coladas) and the spot for an education by some of the finest percussionists in Miami. Pocho was the anchor, the Quarterback, and music director of what became known as the "5:00 Rumba." My private education with him launched me into my current career as a musician, author, and educator, and reminiscing on my acceptance from the "players" in town validated Pocho's excellent tutoring.

Having recently met Jose Rosa I initially realized that his genteel demeanor is his personality, but come time to play all reservations are unleashed to the congas and this cat is serious! Noticeably from the Neciosup "school" Jose is an excellent teacher, communicator and superbly talented musician. Together these two gentleman have written the comprehensive book you are about to dive into. Practice routines, exercises, tuning, hand techniques and authentic rhythms are all revealed. We can never stop learning regardless of ability, so I am confident that the messages relayed to you in the upcoming pages will progress your conga chops to the next level...It already has for me!

Glen Caruba

Preface

First and foremost, I would like to thank my Lord and Savior Jesus Christ for the new life that he had given me in him. I want to thank my students and all of those who inspire me daily to keep growing as an individual and as a teacher. To my friend Giovanni Hidalgo, thank you for inspiring me to do this. Thanks to my dear friend Professor Jose "Pepe" Torres for your guidance and counseling. To my wife Maria and my children Elizabeth and Isaac, thank you for your continuous support and Love. To Pochito, thanks for accepting the challenge of doing this book together. God Bless you,

Primeramente, quiero agradecer a mi Señor y Salvador Jesucristo por haberme dado una nueva vida en El. Quiero agradecer a todos mis estudiantes y a todos aquellos que me inspiran diariamente a seguir creciendo como individuo y como educador. A mi amigo Giovanni Hidalgo por inspirarme a hacer este proyecto. A quien considero como mi Papa y quien me llevo debajo de sus alas durante el periodo mas difícil de mi vida, me instruyo, me aconsejo y gracias a el soy quien soy, esa persona es el Profesor José "Pepe" Torres. A mi esposa Maria y a mis hijos, Elizabeth y Isaac; por su apoyo incondicional y lo mas importante por su amor para mi. Ustedes son bien especiales para mí y doy gracias a Dios por ustedes a diario. A mi gran hermano y amigo "Pocho", gracias por haber aceptado el reto de hacer este libro juntos, eres como un hermano para mí. Que el Señor los continúe Bendiciendo,

Jose "Miguel" Rosa

First of all, I would like to thank my Lord and Savior Jesus Christ for salvation and for helping me discover my natural and spiritual talents. He is the reason why I write these pages. I would like to thank my dad Moises Neciosup (R.I.P.) for your influence and your support in all the aspects of my life, I miss you dad. At the same time, I would like to thank my wife Sandra and my daughters Stephanie and Sara for their continual support. I want to thank my uncle Alex Neciosup Acuna (Alex Acuna) for your inspiration and help. To my friend Jose Rosa, Thank you for your sincere friendship, you are like a brother to me and you have shown me the love of God with your life. Blessings to all,

Primeramente, quiero agradecer al mi Señor y Salvador Jesucristo por su salvación y por haberme ayudado a descubrir mis talentos naturales y espirituales. El es la razón por las cuales escribo estas páginas. Quisiera agradecer a mi papa Moises Neciosup (Q.D.P.) por su influencia y su apoyo en todos los aspectos de mi vida, Te extraño mucho papi. A la misma vez quisiera agradecer a mi esposa Sandra y mis hermosas hijas Stephanie y Sara por su apoyo incondicional. Quiero agradecer a mi tío Alex Neciosup Acuña por su inspiración, su amor y su apoyo incondicional para conmigo. A mi gran amigo José Rosa, gracias por tu sincera amistad, tu eres como un hermano para mi y me has mostrado el amor de Dios a través de tu vida.

Hector "Pocho" Neciosup

About the Authors

Photo Courtesy of Hector "Pocho" Neciosup (http://www.myspace.com/pochoneciosup)

Héctor "Pocho" Neciosup

Born and raised in Lima, Perú. Héctor comes from a well known family of musicians his grandfather Fernando Neciosup, his dad Moises Neciosup Acuña both distinguished music teachers in Peru. But the person that inspired him the most was his uncle, Alejandro Neciosup Acuña (Alex Acuña) world renowned percussionist. Hector was introduced to percussion instruments from a very early age and by age seven he had mastered the basic beats for those instruments .At age fifteen, Hector was accepted at the Conservatory of music in Lima Peru. At age eighteen, he moved to the United States and participated in a drum contest directed by the legendary Louis Bellson, in which he won the first place. Consequently, Hector was granted a full scholarship to study at the University of Miami with Professor Steve Bagby and Professor Steve Rucker. During that period he was part of the faculty as Latin Percussion Instructor for Miami Institute of Percussion, which was founded by Russ Miller.

Through the course of his life, Hector has had the opportunity to perform and tour with major recording artists such as "Trumpet Virtuoso" Arturo Sandoval, Paquito D'Rivera, Alex Acuna and The Unknowns, Justo Almario, Eva Ayllon, Michael Brecker, Mongo Santamaria, Bob James, Eddie Daniels, Tania Maria, Nestor Torres, Mike Orta and Willy Chirino. He has also performed with several Christian recording artists such as Richie Ray, Grupo Nueva Vida, Bobby Cruz, Tom Brooks, Don Moen, Ingrid Rosario, Ricardo Rodriguez and Danilo Montero.

Presently, he is currently working with founder member of Cuban legendary band "Irakere" Mr. Carlos Averhoff and had recorded on his latest album entitled: "Jazz 'ta Bueno" (Universal Music). In addition, Hector has been on faculty at Florida International University for the past 10 years. Presently, Hector is one of the most sought after music teacher and performer in Miami, FL.

Photo Courtesy of Jose Rosa (http://www.myspace.com/josemrosa)

 José Rosa

Born and raised in Humacao, Puerto Rico, Jose has been performing on percussion instruments since he was five years old. At age 11, he started formal music lessons with Professor Jose "Tito" Rivera at the Escuela Libre De Música de Humacao. At 12 years of age, Jose started performing with Humacao Symphonic Band under the direction of Professor German Peña Plaza. With the Humacao Symphonic Band, Jose traveled to Venezuela, New York, Costa Rica, Virgin Islands and Dominican Republic. At age 14, Jose received formal percussion lessons from Professor Jose "Pepe" Torres at the Escuela Libre de Música de Caguas. Under Torres direction, Jose performed with the Puerto Rico Symphony Orchestra, Puerto Rico State Band and also with a variety of local bands. By the age of 17, Jose was accepted into the Puerto Rico Conservatory of Music where he studied percussion with Professor Jose Alicea. Under Alicea's direction, Jose played for the America youth symphony orchestra based in San Juan, Puerto Rico. In 1994, Jose moved to Miami, where he attended the University of Miami and Florida International University.

Through the course of his life, Jose has had the opportunity to perform with renown artists such as "Trumpet Virtuoso" - Arturo Sandoval, "El Maestro" Tito Puente, Mike Orta, Bobby Cruz, "Steel Pan virtuoso" Liam Teague, Marcos Barrientos, Danilo Montero. He had also performed at the Disney's Animal Kingdom "Tarzan Rocks" and "The Village Beatniks" shows, at the Universal Studios Florida "The I Love Lucy tribute show!", "Orlando Sanchez and Akangana", "Rico Monaco and Sol Sons", "Michael Andrews & Swingerhead" and he can also be seen on the show "The Making of Disney's Animal Kingdom" on the Travel Channel. Checkout Jose's MYSPACE Page located at: http://www.myspace.com/josemrosa. Jose currently resides in Orlando, Florida where he performs, does recordings and also teaches percussion on a regular basis.

Introduction

During our years of performing and educating, we have learned that the key to developing good techniques on hand drums is to use practical strengthening exercises coupled with lots of repetition to develop the speed, independence and control needed to become a good Hand drummer. Therefore, our goal is to help you develop a good sound by incorporating strengthening exercises coupled with various techniques to develop your strength, speed, independence and control needed. This book was written to provide quick and to the point lessons so that you can take it with you and use it as a reference guide wherever you are. This book is designed for the hand drummer that is eager to step to the next level in performance. We have included some practical exercises for coordination and independence that will help you increase your level of performance. Regardless of whether you are looking to develop more strength, more speed or soloing, this book answers many questions you might have in regards to advance techniques and independence. We invite you also to check our **website: http://www.clmeducators.com**, for more information. It is our hope to pass on the knowledge and experience we have gained over the years studying and playing professionally in a way that can easily be understood to inspire the next generation of conga players.

Hector Neciosup & Jose Rosa

CHAPTER ONE
Beyond "La Mano Secreta"

Después de "La Mano Secreta"

Beyond "La Mano Secreta"?

The following chapter will set the foundation for the rest of this book. Many of our students after they had mastered some of the basic "Mano Secreta" exercises ask us: *What's Next?* Our answer is very simple: "We will continue working on practical exercises but this time implementing exercises to develop coordination and independence". For some people, this is a very easy task but for most people it is a battle. That is the reason behind this chapter; we want it to address this issue that for most people is a *major challenge.* Start practicing these exercises very slowly and increase speed gradually.

Let's start with the exercises:

El próximo capitulo va a crear el fundamento para el resto de el libro. Muchos de nuestros estudiantes luego de haber dominado los ejercicios básicos de "La Mano Secreta" nos preguntan: *"Bueno y ahora que viene luego?"* Nuestra respuesta es simple: *"Vamos a continuar trabajando en ejercicios prácticos, pero esta vez le vamos a añadir ejercicios para desarrolla coordinación e independencia"* Para muchas personas es una tarea fácil, pero para otros es un reto. Por esa razón decidimos escribir este capitulo. Comienza estudiando estos ejercicios lentos e incremente la velocidad de manera gradual.

Comencemos con los ejercicios:

Keep practicing these exercises on a daily basis, even if you master them. It is always a good idea to practice this on a solo situation, also you can mix and match different exercises. Let's move to our next chapter, "Rudiments: Exercises to develop independence."

CHAPTER TWO

"Rudiments: Exercises to develop independence"

Rudimentos: Ejercicios para desarrollar independencia

"Flam Paradiddle"

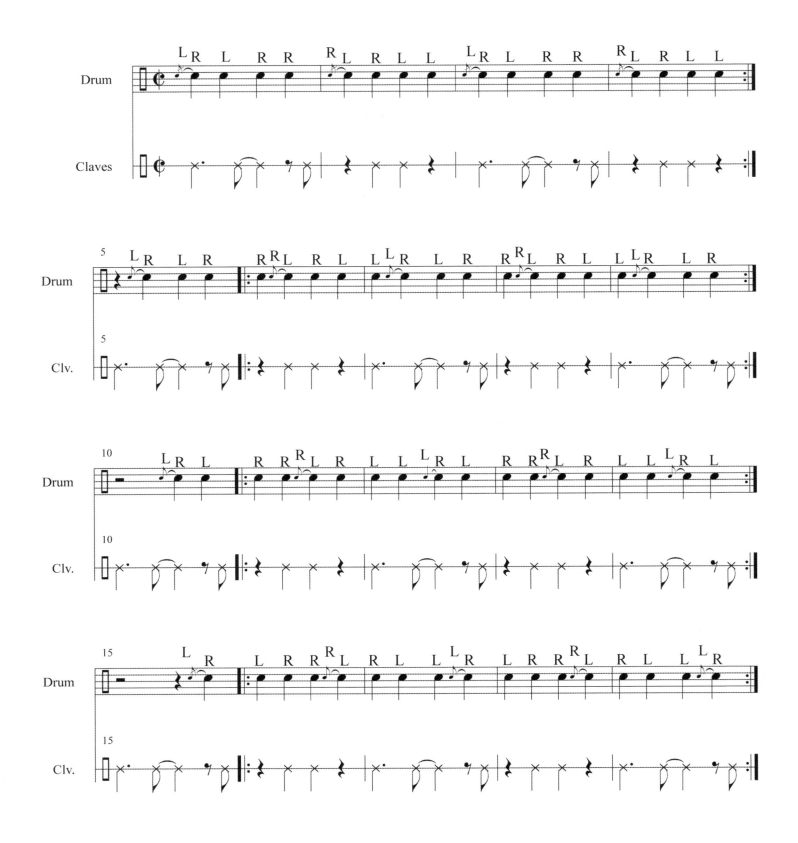

"Flam Paradiddle Exercise-2"

These exercises are to be practice slowly first and start increasing speed gradually.

"Double Flam Paradiddle"

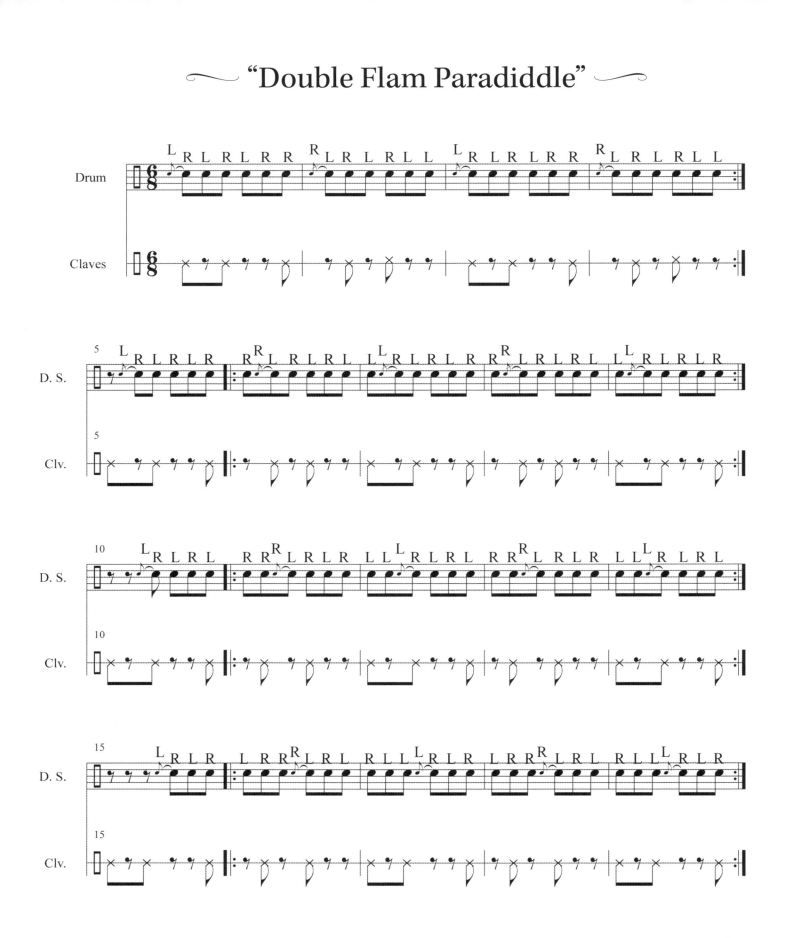

Remember to start working on these exercises slowly and increase speed gradually Now, let's work on some snare drum etudes adapted for the hand drums.

"Hand Drums Etudes with clave"

Estudios para "Hand Drum" con la clave

Etude I

Etude II

Etude III

"Afro-Caribbean Rhythms"

Courtesy of CLM Educators, www.clmeducators.com

Ritmos Afro-Caribeños

Guaguanco 3-2 Rumba Clave

Guaguanco (3 Congas)

Playing 3-2 clave at the same time

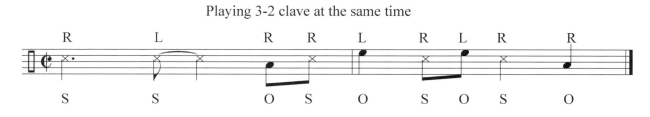

Comparsa 3 congas

Songo

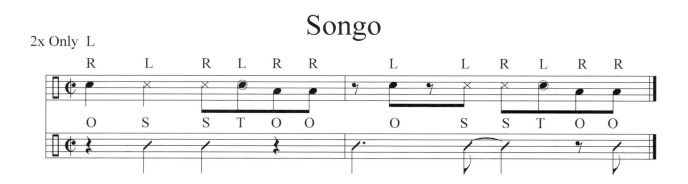

Plena

(2 Congas) ver 1.

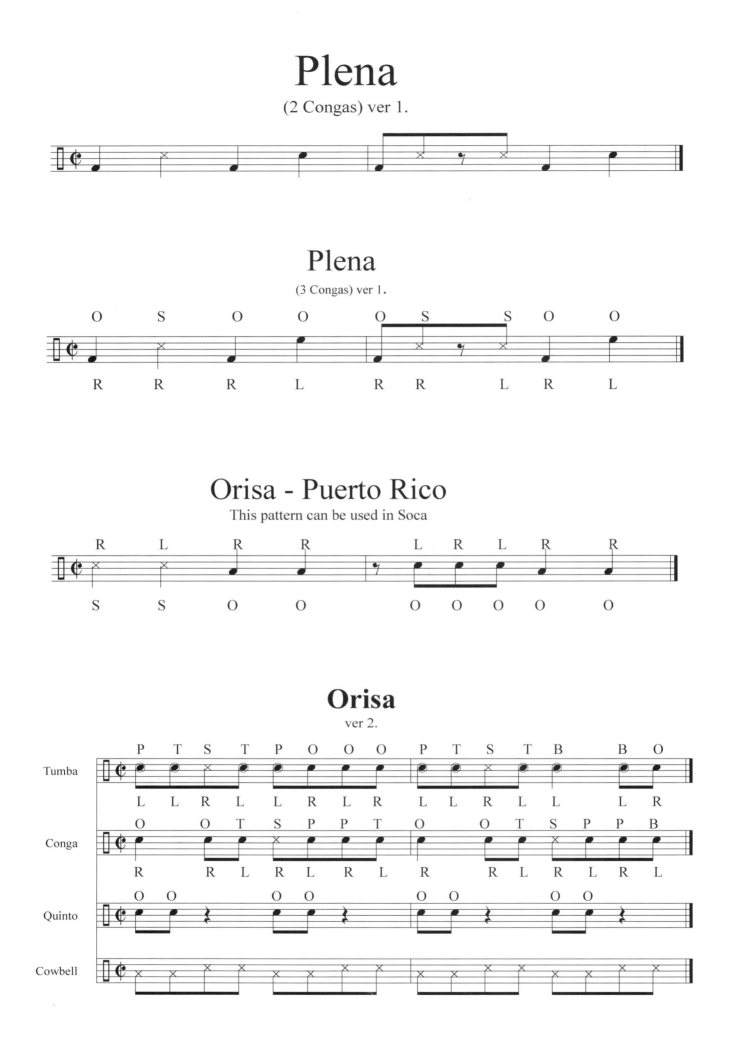

Plena

(3 Congas) ver 1.

Orisa - Puerto Rico

This pattern can be used in Soca

Orisa

ver 2.

Afro-Rican 6/8

Mozambique

Rumba Columbia

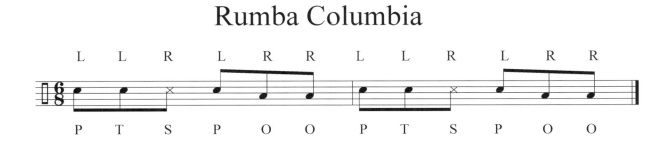

Pilon

Abakua for 3 congas

Yambu

Cumbia

Merengue

Merengue a lo Maco

Tumbao en 7

Tumbao en 9

American Pop-Rock

⌒ Conclusion ⌒

In summary, we have worked on aspects using "La Mano Secreta" and develop it to achieve a different level of performance. We hope this book has been a blessing for you and we pray that God will give you the wisdom and understanding that you need to develop musically. Check out our website: http://www.clmeducators.com, if you are just a beginning musician, keep doing the work, practice, practice, practice and create your own style. If you are a professional musician, keep doing the work. We want to wish you the best of luck in this business and remember that if you don't understand something we are always available for private and/or group lessons. God Bless you,

Hemos trabajado en algunos aspectos utilizando "La Mano Secreta" y desarrollándola para alcanzar un nivel más alto de ejecución. Esperamos que este libro haya sido de bendición para ti y oramos que Dios abra tu mente para poder entender este concepto. Visita nuestro Web-site http://www.clmeducators.com, para más información. Te queremos desear mucha suerte en este negocio y recuerde que si no entiende algo estamos disponibles para clases privadas o clases grupales.

Dios Los Bendiga,

Hector Neciosup & Jose Rosa

⌒ Credits ⌒

Executive Producers: Ron Middlebrook, Jose Rosa and Hector "Pocho" Neciosup for Centerstream Publishing

Music Producers: Jose Rosa and Hector "Pocho" Neciosup

Audio Production: Contemporary Latin Music Educators for Centerstream Publishing

Audio Engineers: Andrés García, José Rosa, Héctor Neciosup & José Acosta

Mastering: Acosta Productions (José Acosta)

Music Performed by: "Tinya" - Featuring Hector "Pocho" Neciosup – Conga Solo, Timbales, Guiro, Cua. And Jose Rosa – Conga Solo, Bongo and Bongo Cowbell .